FLORENCE
CITY CENTER

0 km   50

0 miles   50

D0375992

EYEWITNESS TRAVEL

FLORENCE

POCKET
GUIDE

LONDON, NEW YORK,
MELBOURNE, MUNICH AND DELHI
www.dk.com

PROJECT DIRECTORS Nicholas Bevan, Derek Hall

EDITORS Viv Croot, Sue Juby

DESIGNER Tony Truscott

INDEXER Michael Dent

PICTURE RESEARCHER Mirco De Cet

CARTOGRAPHY John Plumer

Conceived and produced by Redback Publishing, 25 Longhope
Drive, Farnham, Surrey, GU10 4SN

Reproduced by Colourscan (Singapore)

Printed and bound by Leo Paper Products Ltd.

First published in Great Britain in 2006
by Dorling Kindersley Limited
80 Strand, London WC2R 0RL

Reprinted with revisions 2008

**The information in this
DK Eyewitness Travel Guide is checked regularly.**
Every effort has been made to ensure that this book is as up-to-date as
possible at the time of going to press. Some details, however, such as
telephone numbers, opening hours, prices, gallery hanging
arrangements and travel information, are liable to change. The
publishers cannot accept responsibility for any consequences arising
from the use of this book, nor for any material on third-party websites,
and cannot guarantee that any website address in this book will be a
suitable source of travel information. We value the views and
suggestions of our readers highly. Please write to:
Publisher, DK Eyewitness Travel Guides,
Dorling Kindersley, 80 Strand, London WC2R 0RL.

View across to San Miniato al Monte from Forte di Belvedere

CONTENTS

Triumphal Arch in Piazza della Repubblica, Florence

Florence

The sights described in this book are grouped within four areas. The centre is focused on the massive Duomo. Santa Croce to the east, San Marco to the north, Santa Maria Novella to the west and the Palazzo Pitti in Oltrarno mark the outlying areas.

City Centre West
*Ponte Santa Trinità,
with Ponte Vecchio
seen (see pp40–1).*

VIALE FILIPPO STROZZI

VIA

PIAZZA DE
INDIPENDE

PIAZZA DEL
CROCIFISSO

VIA

GUEL

FS PIAZZA DELLA
STAZIONE

Cappelle
Medice

Santa Maria
Novella

San
Lorenzo

VIA DELLA SCALA

Bibliotec
Medicec
Laurenzi

Ponte A.
Vespucci

LAM. VESPUCCI

LUNGARNO SODERINI

BORGO SAN FREDIANO

PIAZZA
CARLO
GOLDONI

VIGNA NUOVA

VIA DE' TORNABUONI

PIAZZA DELL
REPUBBLICA

PIAZZA
NAZARIO
SAURO

Ponte alla
Carraia

Ponte
S. Trinita

LUNG. D.
ACCIAIUOLI

Arno

PIAZZA DEL
CARMINE

VIA SANTO SPIRITO

PIAZZA DE
S. FELICITA

Pont
Vecc

PIAZZA
TORQUATO
TASSO

Cappella
Brancacci
(Santa Maria

VIA DEL CAMPUCCIO

VIA DE' SERRAGLI

V. S. AGOSTINO

PIAZZA
SANTO
SPIRITO

VIA

PIAZZA
DE' PITTI

Palazzo
Pitti

GIARDINO
TORRIGIANI

PIAZZA
DI SAN
FELICE

VIALE FRANCESCO PETRARCA

VIA ROMANA

GIARDINO DI
BOBOLI

PIAZZALE DELLA
PORTA ROMANA

0 metres   500

0 yards   500

City Centre North
Fountain in Piazza della Santissima Annunziata
(see p34).

City Centre East
The main entrance to Palazzo Vecchio
(see pp22–3).

KEY

▮	Major sight
FS	Railway station
🚌	Bus terminus
🚍	Coach terminus
🚋	Tram station (due to open 2007/8)

Florence's Highlights

Florence is a compact city and you cannot go far without stumbling across Renaissance architecture and art or projects funded by the powerful Medici, Florence's first family. Below are some of the highlights to look out for if you're on a time budget.

Duomo, Campanile and Baptistry

Churches

The Duomo
If you only see one sight, make it the Duomo. Brunelleschi's dome is unmissable *(see pp12–13)*.

Santa Croce
Tombs of great Florentines (Galileo, Michelangelo), cloisters and chapel by Brunelleschi and frescoes by Giotto and Taddeo Gaddi *(see pp16–17)*.

Santa Maria Novella
Façade by Alberti on the outside; Masaccio's *The Trinity* and Strozzi Chapel on the inside *(see p45)*.

San Lorenzo
The parish church of the Medici, by Brunelleschi; library and tombs by Michelangelo *(see p30–1)*.

Brancacci Chapel
Part of the church of Santa Maria del Carmine; famous for the fresco cycle of *The Life of St Peter* by Masaccio *(see p53)*.

Museums and Galleries

The Uffizi
The oldest art gallery in the world, and the home of iconic paintings such as Botticelli's *The Birth of Venus*, *The Duke and Duchess of Urbino* (Piero della Francesca) and *The Holy Family* (Michelangelo) *(see p24)*.

The Bargello
One of Italy's first national museums. The place to see superb Renaissance sculpture by Donatello, Cellini, Michelangelo, Verrocchio and others *(see p11)*.

Galleria dell'Accademia
The first art school in Europe (founded 1563), now a gallery containing most of Michelangelo's important works, including the *David (see p32)*.

Elegant façade of The Uffizi

Architecture

Palazzo Strozzi
The largest palazzo in
Florence, notable for its
monumental rusticated
blocks *(see p39)*.

Ponte Vecchio
You cannot leave Florence
without strolling across the
Ponte Vecchio, browsing
through its jewellery shops
and admiring the fine view
of the city *(see pp40–1)*.

Spedale degli Innocenti
Europe's first orphanage, a
monument to Renaissance
humanism and the genius
of Brunelleschi *(see p33)*.

Ponte Vecchio

Squares and Gardens

Piazza della Signoria
A wonderful free outdoor
sculpture gallery with the
Palazzo Vecchio, remod-
elled for Cosimo di Medici
by Vasari running along
one side *(see pp20–1)*.

Piazza di San Lorenzo
Dominated by the San
Lorenzo church on the west
side, the square hosts a
busy market for tourists and
locals alike *(see p28)*.

Piazza della Repubblica
One of Florence's few
non-Renaissance piazze,
built in 1890 on the site of
a Roman forum. Impressive
triumphal arch, and great
street life, restaurants and
cafés *(see p43)*.

Piazza di Santa Trinità
Beautiful square lined with
palazzi and leading, on the
south side, to the Ponte
Santa Trinità, with its
stunning view of the
Ponte Vecchio *(see p39)*.

Boboli Gardens
Gardens to the Medici's
Palazzo Pitti, a perfect
example of stylized formal
Renaissance garden design
(see pp50–1).

Famous Florentines

Casa di Dante
Possibly the birthplace of
Dante Alighieri, and not far
from Santa Margherita de'
Cerchi, where the poet first
saw Beatrice *(see p10)*.

Casa Buonarroti
Three modest houses once
owned by Michelangelo
(Buonarroti), now housing
a collection of his work,
including some significant
early pieces *(see p14)*.

**Museo di Storia della
Scienza**
Dedicated to Galileo
Galilei, court mathematician
to the Medici; features live
demonstrations of some of
his experiments *(see p15)*.

Courtyard of Spedale degli
Innocenti

CITY CENTRE EAST

Although Florence was largely rebuilt during the Renaissance, the eastern part of the city, dominated by the great Duomo, retains a distinctly medieval feel. With its confusing maze of tiny alleyways, hidden lanes and artisan workshops, it would still be recognizable to Dante.

SIGHTS AT A GLANCE

Museums and Galleries
The Bargello ⑥
Casa Buonarroti ⑩
Casa di Dante ④
Museo di Firenze com'era ⑧
Museo Horne ⑫
Museo dell'Opera del
   Duomo ②
Museo di Storia della
   Scienza ⑬
Palazzo Nonfinito ⑦
Palazzo Vecchio pp22–3 ⑰
The Uffizi ⑱

Churches
Badia Fiorentina ⑤
*Duomo, Campanile and
   Baptistry pp12–13* ①
Orsanmichele ③
Santa Croce pp16–17 ⑪
Santo Stefano al Ponte ⑭

Historic Streets and Piazzas
*Piazza della Signoria
   pp20–1* ⑯

Shops
Erboristeria ⑮

Ice-cream Parlours
Bar Vivoli Gelateria ⑨

SEE ALSO

• *Street Life p25*

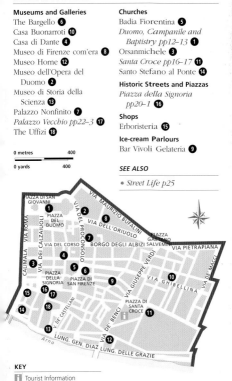

KEY

🛈 Tourist Information

◀ *Michelangelo's David in Piazza della Signoria*

Duomo, Campanile and Baptistry ❶

See pp 12–13.

Carving from della Robbia's choir loft in the Museo dell'Opera del Duomo

Museo dell'Opera del Duomo ❷

Map 4F. Piazza del Duomo. Open daily except 25 Dec, 1 Jan, Easter Sun. Adm charge.

The museum houses pieces taken out of the Duomo over the centuries, as well as tools used by Brunelleschi's workmen, a copy of Arnolfo di Cambio's original cathedral façade and statues from his workshop. There are also works by Pisano, della Robbia and Donatello, and a Michelangelo *Pietà* intended for his own tomb.

Bust of Dante on the façade of Casa di Dante

Orsanmichele ❸

Map 4E. Via dell'Arte della Lana. Open Tue–Sun except 25 Dec, 1 Jan, 1 May. Free.

The name is a corruption of Orto di San Michele, St Michael's garden. Orsanmichele was built in 1337 as a grain market on the site of a former monastery garden, but then became a church. Along the outside walls are 14 niches, each holding a statue of the patron saint of one of Florence's major *Arti* (guilds). Inside is an ornate 1350s altar by Andrea Orcagna, covered in cherubs and carved reliefs. Close to this is Bernardo Daddi's *Virgin and Child* (1348). Orsanmichele is temporarily closed. Call ahead of your visit.

St George on the façade of Orsanmichele

Casa di Dante ❹

Map 4E. Via Santa Margherita. Open Tue–Sun except last Sun of month. Adm charge.

Dante Alighieri (1265–1321) may not actually have been born here, but it is a genuine 13th-century tower house restored in 1911. North of the house is the 11th-century parish church of Santa Margherita de' Cerchi, where Dante is said to have first caught sight of Beatrice Portinari, whom he idolized in his poetry. The church, used for Baroque chamber concerts, has a fine altarpiece by Neri di Bicci (1418–91).

The Virgin Appearing to St Bernard (1485) by Filippino Lippi

Badia Fiorentina ❺

Map 4E. Via del Proconsolo. Open 3–6pm Mon. Free.

One of Florence's oldest churches, the abbey was founded in 978 by Willa, widow of Count Uberto of Tuscany. It contains many 15th-century tombs, including that of her son Count Ugo, carved by Mino da Fiesole almost 500 years after the Count's death in 1001. Mino also carved the altarpiece and the tomb of Bernardo Guigni, the Florentine statesman. Other must-sees are Filippino Lippi's *The Virgin Appearing to St Bernard* (1485); the two-tier cloister, built by Rossellino in 1435–40, with its fresco cycle of the scenes from the life of St Benedict; and an early fresco by Bronzino (1503–72). The hexagonal campanile is mentioned by Dante in *The Divine Comedy*. The poet

Boccaccio (1313–75) used to give readings and lectures on Dante's work here in the 14th century. Today, the abbey is still used for talks and concerts.

The Bargello ❻

Map 4F. Via del Proconsolo. Open daily except 25 Dec, 1 Jan, 1 May, 2nd & 4th Mon & 1st, 3rd & 5th Sun of mth. Adm charge.

Built in 1255 as the city's town hall, the Bargello is the oldest seat of government surviving in Florence. In the 16th century it was the residence of the chief of police and a prison: executions took place here until 1786. After extensive renovation, it became one of Italy's first national museums in 1865. There are rooms dedicated to the work of Michelangelo, Donatello, Verrocchio, Giambologna and Cellini, as well as a collection of Mannerist bronzes and examples from the decorative arts. Don't miss Donatello's famous bronze *David* (1450).

Sculpture by Cellini in The Bargello

Duomo, Campanile and Baptistry ❶

Santa Maria del Fiore – the Duomo, or cathedral, of Florence – was begun in 1296 by Arnolfo di Cambio. Many great Florentine artists contributed to it, including Giotto and Pisano, Ghiberti, who created the Baptistry doors, and Filippo Brunelleschi who designed the dome in 1420.

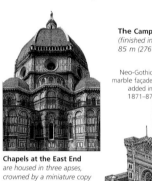

Chapels at the East End
are housed in three apses, crowned by a miniature copy of the dome.

The Campanile
(finished in 1359) is 85 m (276 ft) high.

Neo-Gothic marble façade added in 1871–87

Gothic windows

Main entrance

South doors

Terracotta panels by Andrea Pisano

The Baptistry Ceiling
is decorated with mosaics (finished in 1271) illustrating the Last Judgment.

Brunelleschi's Dome *is 91 m (286 ft) high, with a span of 43 m (138.5 ft), and you can get to the top by climbing 463 steps.*

Bricks *set in a herringbone pattern were copied from the Pantheon in Rome.*

Last Judgment frescoes by Vasari

Entrance to steps to the dome

Octagonal marble sanctuary around the High Altar

The Marble Pavement *dating from the 16th century is laid out as a maze, and is best viewed from above.*

VISITORS' CHECKLIST

Map 4E. Piazza del Duomo. Tel 055 230 28 85. Dome & Crypt open Mon–Sat. Baptistry open daily from noon, 8.30am–2pm Sun. Campanile open daily. All closed 1 Jan, 15 Aug & religious hols. Adm charge. www.operaduomo.firenze.it

Palazzo Nonfinito **7**

Map 4F. Via del Proconsolo. Open Thu–Tue except 25 Dec, 1 Jan, 25 Apr, Easter Sun, 1 May, 15 Aug, 8 Dec. Adm charge.

Italy's first ethnological museum (1869), containing art from Italy's colonies and Captain Cook's voyages.

Bar Vivoli Gelateria

Museo di Firenze com'era **8**

Map 4F. Via dell'Oriuolo. Open Mon–Wed & Sat except 25 Dec, 1 Jan, Easter Sun, 1 May, 15 Aug. Adm charge.

A fascinating collection of drawings, plans and paintings tracing the city's development and the influence of the Medicis. The *Pianta della Catena*, a 19th-century copy of a *c.*1470 woodcut, shows Florence at the height of the Renaissance. A sequence of lunettes (1599) by the Flemish artist Giusto Utens catalogues all the Medici villas and gardens. You can also see city

architect Giuseppe Poggi's scheme to remodel central Florence during its brief stint as the capital of Italy in 1865–71. The scheme was halted after an international outcry.

Bar Vivoli Gelateria **9**

Map 5F. Via Isola delle Stinche. Open Tue–Sun except three weeks in Jan & three weeks in Aug.

Vivoli claims to make the "best ice cream in the world", and the walls of the bar are covered in press clippings from connoisseurs that strongly support this view. The tiny ice-cream parlour stands at the heart of the Santa Croce district, with its narrow alleys, tiny squares, local shops and scores of little workshops where craftsmen make and repair furniture. Via Torta is typical of the area.

Casa Buonarroti **10**

Map 5G. Via Ghibellina. Open Wed–Mon except 25-Dec, 1 Jan, Easter Sun, 25 Apr, 1 May. Adm charge.

Michelangelo (Buonarroti) lived briefly in this group of three houses which he bought as an investment in 1508. It is now home to a significant collection of his works, including his earliest known work, the *Madonna della Scala* (1492) and the design, never used, for the façade of San Lorenzo, shown in a wooden model.

Santa Croce **11**

See pp16–17.

Museo Horne

Museo Horne ⓬

Map 5F. Via de' Benci. Open Mon–Sat except 25–26 Dec, 1 Jan, Easter Sun, Easter Mon, 25 Apr, 1 May, 15 Aug, 1 Nov. Adm charge.

The museum is housed in a Renaissance palazzino (small town house), built in 1489 for the Alberti, a family of wealthy cloth merchants. It contains a small collection of paintings, sculpture and decorative arts left to the city by the English art historian Herbert Percy Horne (1844–1916). Many of the museum's major artefacts are now housed in the Uffizi, but the museum still has Giotto's 13th-century *St Stephen* polyptych, a *Madonna and Child* attributed to Simone Martini (1283–1344) and *Madonna* by Bernardo Daddi (c.1312–48). Horne's collection of Renaissance cooking utensils can be seen in the kitchen, built on the top floor to stop fumes passing through the house.

Museo di Storia della Scienza ⓭

Map 5E. Piazza de' Giudici. Open winter: Mon–Sat & 2nd Sun of mth; summer: Mon–Sat. Closed 8, 25–26 Dec, 1 Jan, 25 Apr, 1 May, 24 Jun, 15 Aug. Adm charge.

The museum is devoted to Galileo Galilei (1564–1642). Exhibits include his telescopes and large-scale reconstructions of his many experiments. The world's first-ever scientific institution, the Accademia del Cimento (Academy for Experimentation) was founded in his memory in 1657; some of the academy's inventions are on show

Armillary sphere of 1564, used to map the stars and planets

here. You can also see 16th- and 17th-century globes made to illustrate the motion of the planets and stars, Lopo Homem's map of the world (1554) and the nautical instruments invented by Sir Robert Dudley, the English marine engineer employed by the Medici dukes to build the harbour at Livorno (1607–21).

Santa Croce ⓫

This Gothic church (1294) houses the tombs of
Michelangelo, Machiavelli, Galileo and Lorenzo
Ghiberti and his sons, and contains 14th-century
frescoes by Giotto and Taddeo Gaddi and
magnificent crucifixes by Donatello and Cimabue.

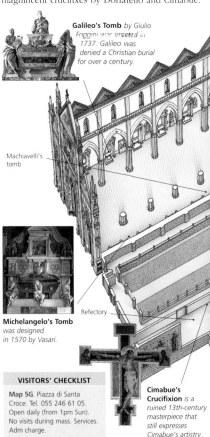

Galileo's Tomb by Giulio
Foggini was erected in
1737. Galileo was
denied a Christian burial
for over a century.

Machiavelli's
tomb

Michelangelo's Tomb
was designed
in 1570 by Vasari.

Refectory

Cimabue's
Crucifixion is a
ruined 13th-century
masterpiece that
still expresses
Cimabue's artistry.

VISITORS' CHECKLIST

Map 5G. Piazza di Santa
Croce. Tel. 055 246 61 05.
Open daily (from 1pm Sun).
No visits during mass. Services.
Adm charge.

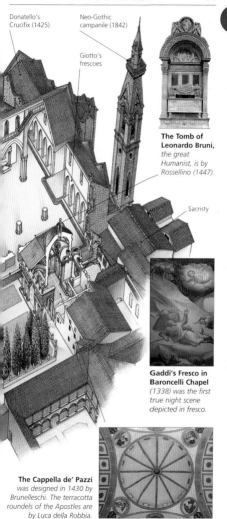

Donatello's Crucifix (1425)

Neo-Gothic campanile (1842)

Giotto's frescoes

The Tomb of Leonardo Bruni, *the great Humanist, is by Rossellino (1447).*

Sacristy

Gaddi's Fresco in Baroncelli Chapel *(1338) was the first true night scene depicted in fresco.*

The Cappella de' Pazzi *was designed in 1430 by Brunelleschi. The terracotta roundels of the Apostles are by Luca della Robbia.*

Piazza della Signoria 16

The piazza, with the Palazzo Vecchio (see pp22–3), has been at the heart of Florentine politics since the 14th century. Citizens gathered in the square when called to a *parlamento* (a public meeting) by the Palazzo's great bell, and Savonarola was burned at the stake here in 1498.

Salone dei Cinquecento, *built in 1495, is decorated with Vasari's frescoes depicting the history of Florence.*

Palazzo Vecchio

Grand Duke of Tuscany *Cosimo I (1519–74) celebrated in a marble statue by Giambologna (1595).*

VISITORS' CHECKLIST

Map 5E. Pedestrian area.

◀ *Detail from the east doors of the Baptistry*

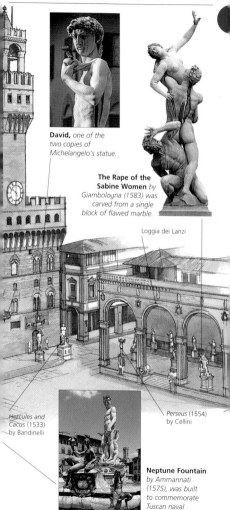

David, *one of the two copies of Michelangelo's statue.*

The Rape of the Sabine Women *by Giambologna (1583) was carved from a single block of flawed marble.*

Loggia dei Lanzi

Perseus (1554) by Cellini

Hercules and Cacus (1533) by Bandinelli

Neptune Fountain *by Ammannati (1575), was built to commemorate Tuscan naval victories.*

Palazzo Vecchio ⑰

The Palazzo Vecchio ("Old Palace") was
completed in 1322 when the bell, used to call
citizens to meetings or warn of disaster, was
hauled to the top of the belltower. Much of the
interior was remodelled for Duke Cosimo I when
he moved into the palace in 1540. Leonardo and
Michelangelo were invited, but Vasari finally
undertook the work. His many frescoes (1563–5)
glorify Cosimo and the Grand Duchy of Tuscany.

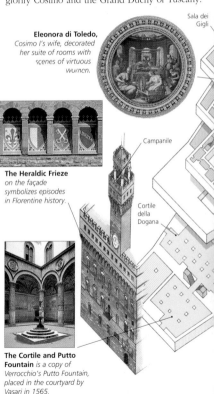

Sala dei Gigli

Eleonora di Toledo,
*Cosimo I's wife, decorated
her suite of rooms with
scenes of virtuous
women.*

The Heraldic Frieze
*on the façade
symbolizes episodes
in Florentine history.*

Campanile

Cortile
della
Dogana

**The Cortile and Putto
Fountain** *is a copy of
Verrocchio's Putto Fountain,
placed in the courtyard by
Vasari in 1565.*

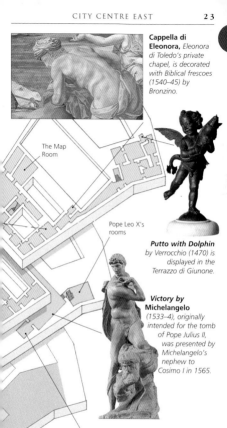

Cappella di Eleonora, *Eleonora di Toledo's private chapel, is decorated with Biblical frescoes (1540–45) by Bronzino.*

The Map Room

Pope Leo X's rooms

Putto with Dolphin *by Verrocchio (1470) is displayed in the Terrazzo di Giunone.*

Victory by Michelangelo *(1533–4), originally intended for the tomb of Pope Julius II, was presented by Michelangelo's nephew to Cosimo I in 1565.*

Museum entrance   The Treasury of Cosimo I

KEY TO FLOORPLAN

- Ground floor
- First floor
- Mezzanine floor
- Second floor
- Temporary exhibition space
- Non-exhibition space

VISITORS' CHECKLIST

Map 5E. Piazza della Signoria. Tel 055 276 82 24. Open daily. The Secret Routes open Mon–Fri except 25 Dec, 1 Jan, Easter, 1 May, 15 Aug. Adm charge.

Santo Stefano al Ponte ⑭

Map 5E. Piazza Santo Stefano al Ponte. Varied opening times. Free.

St Stephen "by the bridge", which dates to 969, is so-called because of its close proximity to the Ponte Vecchio. Its most important architectural feature is the Romanesque façade (1233). Today the church is a venue for orchestral concerts.

Bronze boar in Mercato Nuovo

Erboristeria ⑮

Map 5E. Spezieria–Erboristeria Palazzo Vecchio, Via Vaccchereccia. Open Mon–Sat, 1st & last Sun of month except public hols.

This ancient herbalist's shop, known as Palazzo Vecchio, has a lovely frescoed interior. It sells a range of herbal products made to ancient recipes by monks and nuns. Around the corner at Calimala 4r is the Erboristeria della Antica Farmacia del Cinghiale (Herbalist at the Old Boar Pharmacy), it takes its name from the famous bronze boar statue in the Mercato Nuovo opposite.

Piazza della Signoria ⑯

See pp20–1.

Palazzo Vecchio ⑰

See pp22–3.

The Uffizi ⑱

Map 5E. Loggiato degli Uffizi. Open Tue–Sat except 25 Dec, 1 Jan, 1 May. Adm charge.

The Uffizi was built in 1560–80 as a suite of offices (*uffici*) for Duke Cosimo I's new administration. The architect, Vasari, used iron reinforcement to create an almost continuous wall of glass on the upper storey. From 1581 Cosimo's heirs used this well-lit space to display the Medici family art treasures, creating what is now the oldest art gallery in the world. The gallery houses important collections of Gothic, Early Renaissance, High Renaissance and Mannerist art, as

Arno façade of The Uffizi with the Vasari Corridor above

The Birth of Venus *(1485) by Sandro Botticelli, from The Uffizi*

well as non-Florentine work
Important paintings include
The Ognissanti Madonna
(1310) by Giotto, *The Duke
and Duchess of Urbino*
(1460) by Piero della
Francesca, Botticelli's *The
Birth of Venus* (1485), *The
Holy Family* (1507) by
Michelangelo and Titian's
The Venus of Urbino (1538).
The Tribune (Room 18),
with its mother of pearl
ceiling, was designed by
Buontalenti in 1584 so that
Francesco I could display all
his favourite works in one
room. These paintings are
hung in a series of rooms
off the main corridor, in
chronological order, to
show the development of
Florentine art from Gothic to
Renaissance and beyond.
Most of the best-known
paintings are in rooms 7–18.
The Arno corridor, linking
the east and west wings, is
lined with the Medici's
collection of ancient Roman
statues, and offers fine views
of the hills to the south of
Florence. To avoid queues,
book your ticket in advance.
Disruptions are possible
during building works.

STREET LIFE

RESTAURANTS

I Buongustai
Map 4E. Via dei Cerchi 15r.
Tel 055 291 304.
Cheap
*Traditional Tuscan fare as well
as crepes and great desserts.*

Acqua al Due
Map 4F. Via della Vigna
Vecchia 40r. Tel 055 284 170.
Moderate
*Dinner only, but assaggi (tast-
ing) dishes to try each course.*

See page 80 for price codes.

BARS

I Fratellini
Map 4E. Via dei Cimatori 38r.
*Traditional fiaschetteria. Hole-
in-the-wall wine bar serving
delicious sandwiches to go.*

SHOPPING

**Leather School of Santa
Croce**
Map 5G. Piazza di Santa Croce
(inside church).
*High-quality, butter-soft
leather goods. Artisans will
personalize your purchase in
gold leaf while you wait.*

CITY CENTRE NORTH

This area is stamped with the character of Cosimo il Vecchio, the man who founded the great Medici dynasty. Cosimo wanted the churches, palazzi and libraries that he built to last a thousand years, like the buildings of ancient Rome. To this end, he commissioned some of the greatest architects and artists of the time to build the churches of San Lorenzo and San Marco, and the Palazzo Medici Riccardi.

SIGHTS AT A GLANCE

KEY

🛈 Tourist information

◀ *The Biblioteca Riccardiana in the Palazzo Medici Riccardi*

Mercato Centrale food market

Mercato Centrale ❶

Map 2D. Via dell'Ariento. Open Mon–Sat.

At the heart of the San Lorenzo street market is Florence's busiest food market, the Mercato Centrale. Built in 1874, it is packed with fish, meat and cheese stalls downstairs, while fruit and vegetables are sold upstairs beneath the glass and cast-iron roof. Get your receipts stamped to benefit from reduced-rate parking in the 24-hour car park.

San Lorenzo street market

San Lorenzo ❷

See pp30–1.

Piazza di San Lorenzo ❸

Map 3E. Market open daily except Mon in winter.

Market stalls stretch all the way up the side of San Lorenzo church and into the streets leading off the piazza. The stalls closest to the church cater mostly for tourists. The neighbouring shops have become an integral part of the market, selling cheeses, hams, home-baked bread, pastries, fabrics and table linen.

Statue of Giovanni delle Bande Nere in Piazza di San Lorenzo

Palazzo Pucci ❹

Map 3E. Via de' Pucci. Closed to the public.

The Palazzo Pucci is the ancestral home of the late clothes designer Emilio Pucci, Marchese di Barsento. The Pucci family, traditionally friends and allies of the Medici, features prominently in Florence's history, and this large palace was built in the 16th century to designs by Bartolomeo Ammannati. Emilio Pucci's boutique is at Via Tornabuoni 22r. Haute-couture clients were fitted out in the palatial rooms above the showroom. Pucci is most famous for smart but casual clothes, and designed the stylish blue uniforms worn by Florentine traffic police, the *vigili urbani*.

Palazzo Medici Riccardi ❺

Map 3E. Via Cavour. Capella dei Magi open Thu–Tue except 25 Dec, 1 May. Adm charge.

Once home to the Medici for 100 years, from 1444 to 1544, the palazzo was later acquired by the Riccardi family and now houses government offices. It was built to an austere design by Michelozzo for Cosimo il Vecchio. Only a few rooms in the palazzo are open to the public, including the Cappella dei Magi which houses Benozzi Gozzoli's *The Procession of the Magi* (1459–60), and the Sala di Luca Giordano. A selection of sculptures from the Medici Riccardi collection is on display in a recently renovated wing. The palazzo often hosts temporary art exhibitions, for which there is an additional charge.

Cenacolo di Sant' Apollonia ❻

Map 2E. Via XXVII Aprile. Open daily except 1st, 3rd & 5th Sun, 2nd & 4th Mon of the month. Free.

The cloister and refectory of what was originally a convent for the Camaldolite order of nuns are now used by the students of Florence University. On the main wall of the refectory is a fresco of *The Last Supper* (1445–50), one of the few surviving works by Andrea del Castagno, a pupil of Masaccio and early experimenter with perspective.

Statuary in the garden of the Palazzo Medici Riccardi

San Marco ❼

Map 2F. Piazza di San Marco. Church open daily. Museum open daily except 2nd & 4th Mon & 1st, 3rd & 5th Sun of month, 25 Dec, 1 Jan, 1 May. Adm charge.

The convent of San Marco was founded in the 13th century and enlarged in 1437 when Dominican monks from nearby Fiesole moved here at the invitation of Cosimo il Vecchio. The architect was Cosimo's favourite, Michelozzo. It is now a museum housing Savonarola's cell and the spiritual paintings of Fra Angelico (1395–1455).

San Lorenzo ②

San Lorenzo was the parish church of the Medici family, and they lavished their wealth on it. Brunelleschi rebuilt it in the Renaissance Classical style in 1419. In 1520, Michelangelo began work on the Medici tombs and then created Lorenzo di Medici's library.

Cappella dei Principi, *the Medici mausoleum, contains marble decoration that was not completed until 1962.*

Old Sacristy designed by Brunelleschi and Donatello

The Martyrdom of St Lawrence *by Bronzino (1659) is a study of the human form in various contorted poses.*

Michelangelo's Staircase (1559) leads to the Medici Library.

VISITORS' CHECKLIST

Map 3E. Piazza di San Lorenzo (Basilica and Biblioteca), Piazza di Madonna degli Aldobrandini (Cappelle Medicee). Basilica: tel 055 21 66 34. Open daily. Adm charge. Biblioteca: tel 055 21 07 60 (call to check times). Open Apr–Jun & during exhibitions. Cappelle Medicee: Tel 055 238 86 02 (055 29 48 83 to book). Open daily except 1st, 3rd & 5th Mon, 2nd & 4th Sun of month. Adm charge.

Formal cloister garden

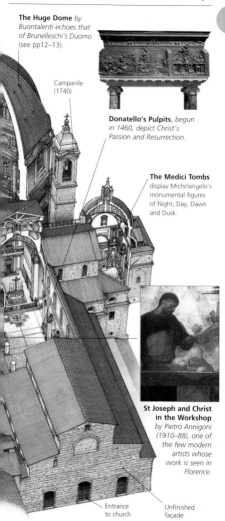

The Huge Dome by Buontalenti echoes that of Brunelleschi's Duomo (see pp12–13).

Campanile (1740)

Donatello's Pulpits, begun in 1460, depict Christ's Passion and Resurrection.

The Medici Tombs display Michelangelo's monumental figures of Night, Day, Dawn and Dusk.

St Joseph and Christ in the Workshop by Pietro Annigoni (1910–88), one of the few modern artists whose work is seen in Florence.

Entrance to church

Unfinished façade

Giardino dei Semplici

Giardino dei Semplici ⑧

Map 2F. Via Micheli. Open
Thu–Tue except 1 Jan, 6 Jan, 25
Apr, Easter Sun & Mon, 1 May,
13–17 Aug, 1 Nov, 24 26 Dec, 31
Dec. Adm charge.

"Semplici" refers to the
"simples" (herbs) used by
medieval apothecaries
to prepare medicine.
This medicinal garden
was set up in 1545 by
Niccolò Tribolo for
Cosimo I. The gar-
den retains its
original layout,
but now has
tropical plants
as well as
Tuscan flora.

Galleria dell'
Accademia ⑨

Map 2F. Via
Ricasoli. Open
Tue–Sun except 25 Dec,
1 Jan, 1 May. Adm charge.

The Academy of Fine
Arts in Florence was
founded in 1563 and
was the first school in
Europe set up to teach
the techniques of
drawing, painting and
sculpture. The art col-
lection displayed in
the gallery was

formed in 1784 with the aim
of providing the students
with material to study and
copy. Many of Michel-
angelo's most important
works are here, with *David*
(1504) being the most
famous them alll. Other
Michelangelo masterpieces
include a statue of St
Matthew (1508), and the
Quattro Prigioni (1521–3)
intended to adorn the tomb
of Pope Julius II. The gallery
contains an important
collection of paintings,
including work by Fra
Bartolomeo, Filippino Lippi,
Agnolo Bronzino and
Ridolfo del Ghirlandajo.
Major works include the
Madonna del Mare,
attributed to Botticelli,
and *Venus and
Cupid* by Jacopo
Pontormo. Also on dis-
play is an elabo-
rately painted
wooden chest,
the *Cassone
Adimari* (c.
1440), by
Scheggia, Masaccio's
step-brother. Much
of the *Salone della
Toscana* (Tuscany
Room) is devoted
to 19th-century
work by members
of the Accademia,
and a series of
original plaster
models by
the sculptor
Lorenzo
Bartolini, pro-
fessor at the
Accademia
from
1839 until
his death
in 1850.

David by Michelangelo

Conservatorio Musicale Luigi Cherubini ⑩

Map 2F. Piazza delle Belle Arti. Library closed to the public.

Some of Italy's finest musicians trained at this musical academy. The conservatory owns a collection of ancient instruments, now on display in the Palazzo Vecchio, acquired by Ferdinando di Medici. It includes violins, violas and cellos by Stradivari, Amati and Ruggeri. There is also a harpsichord by Bartolomeo Cristofori, who invented the piano in the early 18th century, and a fine music library.

Pietre dure *table (1849) by Zocchi.*

Opificio delle Pietre Dure ⑪

Map 3F. Via degli Alfani. Open Mon–Sat except public hols. Adm charge.

The *opificio* (factory), sited in the former monastery of San Niccolò, is a national institute specializing in the Florentine craft of producing inlaid pictures using marble and semi-precious stones. This tradition has flourished since the end of the 16th century, when it was funded through the patronage of the Medici Grand Dukes.

Spedale degli Innocenti ⑫

Map 3F. Piazza della Santissima Annunziata. Open daily except 25 Dec, 1 Jan, Easter. Adm charge.

This "hospital" opened in 1444 as Europe's first orphanage. Brunelleschi's arcaded loggia is decorated with glazed terracotta roundels, added by Andrea della Robbia (c.1498). At the left-hand end of the portico is the *rota*, a rotating stone cylinder on which mothers could place their unwanted children anonymously. The stone was then turned and the child taken in. Inside are two cloisters designed by Brunelleschi, the Men's Cloister (1422–45) and the Women's Cloister (1438), leading to a gallery of work, including Ghirlandaio's *The Adoration of the Magi* (1488), donated by grateful orphans who went on to be successful in later life.

Andrea della Robbia's roundels (c.1490) on the Spedale degli Innocenti

Mannerist fountain by Pietro Tacca in Piazza della Santissima Annunziata

Piazza della Santissima Annunziata ⑬

Map 2F.

The nine-bay arcade on the eastern side of this elegant square was designed by Brunelleschi in 1419, and forms the façade to the Spedale degli Innocenti. An equestrian statue of Duke Ferdinando I by Giambologna dominates the central square. An annual fair is held on the Feast of the Annunciation, 25 March, when home-made sweet biscuits called *brigidini* are sold from the stalls.

Santissima Annunziata ⑭

Map 2F. Piazza della Santissima Annunziata. Open daily. Free.

The Church of the Holy Annunciation was founded by the Servite order in 1250 and rebuilt by Michelozzo between 1444 and 1481. It contains frescoes by Andrea del Sarto, and boasts one of Florence's most revered shrines, a painting of the Virgin Mary begun in 1252 by a monk, and thought to be finished by an angel. A service dedicated to artists is held annually in the Capella di San Luca on St Luke's Day (18 October). The artist Benvenuto Cellini is buried in the vault below.

Museo Archeologico ⑮

Map 2F. Via della Colonna. Open daily except 25-Dec, 1 Jan, 1 May. Adm charge.

Originally a palazzo built for the Maria Maddalena de' Medici in 1620, the museum now houses outstanding collections of Etruscan, Greek, Roman and ancient

The Birth of the Virgin (1514), a fresco by Andrea del Sarto

Egyptian artefacts. There are two famous Etruscan bronzes: the *Chimera,* from the 4th century BC and the *Arringatore* (Orator), from the 1st century BC.

Santa Maria Maddalena dei Pazzi ⓰

Map 3G. Borgo Pinti. Church and Chapterhouse open daily. except for mass 5.30–6pm. Free.

This former convent has been restored following the floods of 1966. Originally run by the Cistercian order, Augustinian monks have lived here since 1926. The unusual portico, with its square-topped, Ionic-style arcades, was designed in 1492 by Giuliano da Sangallo. The chapterhouse contains Perugino's *Crucifixion and Saints* (1493–6). The main chapel, decorated with coloured marble by Ciro Ferri (1675),

is one of the best examples of the High Baroque style.

Tempio Israelitico ⓱

Map 4H. Via Farini. Synagogue and Museum open Sun–Fri except Jewish hols. Free.

The synagogue was built by Marco Treves in 1874–82 in Spanish-Moorish style. It has a museum of ritual objects from the 17th century.

Interior of the Tempio Israelitico

STREET LIFE

RESTAURANTS

Da Mario
Map 2E. Via Rosina 2r.
Tel 055 218 550.
Cheap
This lively trattoria is always packed with customers looking for traditonal homely food. The daily menu features soups, pasta and meat dishes.

Il Vegetario
Map 1E. Via delle Route 30r.
Tel 055 475 030.
Cheap
The decor is rustic and the food wholesome vegetarian. There is a great salad bar.

See page 80 for price codes.

SHOPPING

San Lorenzo Market
Map 2D. Piazza di San Lorenzo.,
A famous outdoor market offering leather goods, fashion items and marbled paper at bargain prices. Closed on Mondays Nov–Feb. The adjacent food market is open every morning except Sunday.

La Botteghina
Map 2D. Via Guelfa 5r.
Excellent examples of hand-painted ceramics from some of central Italy's best artisans. They are open mornings and late afternoons Mon–Fri, mornings only on Sat.

CITY CENTRE WEST

This part of Florence contains the new (the main railway station) and the old (the Ponte Vecchio). There is something to interest most people, from the frescoes of Santa Maria Novella to the Palazzo Strozzi and the Piazza della Repubblica, originally laid out as part of the grandiose plans to remodel Florence when it was briefly the nation's capital. This is also a great shopping area, specializing in leather and fashion.

SIGHTS AT A GLANCE

Museums and Galleries
Museo Marino Marini
  (San Pancrazio) ❶
Museo Nazionale Alinari
  della Fotografia ❶❻
Palazzo Davanzati ❶❶
Palazzo Rucellai ❷

Churches
Ognissanti ❶❼
Santa Maria Novella ❶❽
Santa Trinità ❼
Santi Apostoli ❽

Historic Buildings
Palazzo Antinori ❶❹
Palazzo di Parte Guelfa ❶❶
Palazzo Strozzi ❺
Stazione di Santa
  Maria Novella ❶❾

Historic Streets and Piazzas
Piazza della Repubblica ❶❸
Piazza di Santa Trinità ❻
Via dei Fossi ❶❺
Via de' Tornabuoni ❹
Via della Vigna Nuova ❸

Bridges
Ponte Vecchio pp40–01 ❾

Markets
Mercato Nuovo ❶❷

SEE ALSO

• *Street Life p45*

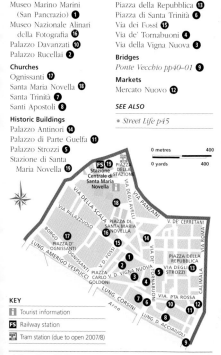

KEY

🅸 Tourist information

FS Railway station

🚊 Tram station (due to open 2007/8)

◀ *Ponte Santa Trinità*

Bronze statue, Cavaliere (1949), by Marini in the Museo Marino Marini

Museo Marino Marini (San Pancrazio) ❶

Map 4D. Piazza San Pancrazio. Open Mon, Wed–Sat except Sat in Jun, Jul, Sep, 1 May, Aug, 25 Dec. Adm charge.

One of the oldest churches in Florence, San Pancrazio was founded in the 9th century but its most attractive features are Renaissance, including the façade and porch (1461–7), and the Capella di San Sepolcro, all by Alberti. Today, the church is a museum devoted to the work of Italy's best-known abstract artist, Marino Marini (1901–80), noted for his bronzes.

Palazzo Rucellai ❷

Map 4D. Via della Vigna Nuova. www.palazzorucellai.com

Built by Alberti in 1446–51, this is one of the most ornate Renaissance palaces in the city. It was commissioned by wealthy cloth merchant Giovanni Rucellai, and is almost a textbook illustration of the major Classical orders. In ascending order of complexity, the pilaster strips on the ground floor are Doric, those above are Ionic and those on the top are Corinthian. On the entablature of the Palazzo entrance you can see the Rucellai's billowing sails of Fortune and the ring symbol of the Medici family. The ring is a reminder that Bernardo Rucellai formed an alliance with the Medici in the 1460s by marrying Lorenzo de' Medici's sister, Lucrezia. The Loggia del Rucellai, opposite the palace, was built to commemorate the marriage. Today the Palazzo remains the property of the Rucellai family.

Via della Vigna Nuova ❸

Map 4D.

The Via della Vigna Nuova is one of Florence's main fashion shopping areas. Many major Italian designers are found here, as well as smaller shops selling luxury silks, cashmeres and lingerie.

La Perla on Via della Vigna Nuova

Exterior of Palazzo Strozzi, with masonry block rustication

Via de' Tornabuoni ❹

Map 4D. Ferragamo Museum. Open Wed–Mon. Adm charge.

Via de' Tornabuoni is the most elegant shopping street in Florence, home to design greats Armani, Prada, Gucci, Bulgari, Cartier and many others. The Ferragamo Museum (No. 2) is dedicated to the work of Florentine shoe designer Salvatore Ferragamo (No. 14r). The medieval tower at the end of the street, now a hotel, used to be a private club for local aristocrats.

Palazzo Strozzi ❺

Map 4D. Piazza degli Strozzi. Open for exhibitions.

The Strozzi palace was commissioned by the wealthy banker and rival to the Medici, Filippo Strozzi, but he died in 1491, two years after the foundation stone was laid. The building was not completed until 1536. It is the biggest palazzo in Florence; 15 buildings were demolished to make way for it, and each of its three storeys is as tall as a normal palazzo. The exterior, built of huge rusticated masonry blocks, remains unspoiled. Look out for the original Renaissance torch-holders, lamps and tethering rings decorating the corners and façades. The palace houses various institutes and the Gabinetto Vieusseux, a 19th-century library. A small vaulted gallery space, La Strozzina, is located at basement level and hosts temporary exhibitions.

Piazza di Santa Trinità ❻

Map 5D.

Noble palazzi line this busy square. To the south is the Palazzo Spini-Ferroni, to the north the Palazzo Bartolini-Salimbeni (1520–29) and, to the west, the Palazzo Corsini (1648–56), a superb example of Florentine Baroque.

Palazzo Spini-Ferroni

Ponte Vecchio ❾

The Ponte Vecchio (Old Bridge) was built in 1345. The butchers, tanners and blacksmiths here originally were evicted in 1593 because of the noise and stench they made. The workshops were rebuilt and let to goldsmiths. Today, the shops lining the bridge still specialize in jewellery.

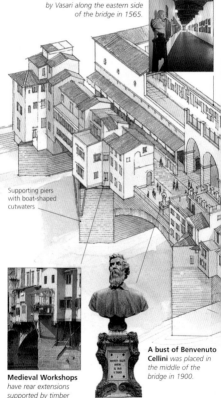

The Private Corridor *was built by Vasari along the eastern side of the bridge in 1565.*

Supporting piers with boat-shaped cutwaters

A bust of Benvenuto Cellini *was placed in the middle of the bridge in 1900.*

Medieval Workshops *have rear extensions supported by timber brackets called sporti.*

The Bridge *looks beautiful seen at sunset from the Ponte Santa Trinità.*

The Manelli Tower *was built as a defence in medieval times.*

Oculi, or circular windows

Jewellers' Shops *sell modern and antique jewellery.*

VISITORS' CHECKLIST

Map 5D. Pedestrian area.

Santa Trinità 7

Map 5D. Piazza di Santa Trinità. Open daily. Free.

The original church, built in the late 11th century by the Vallombrosan monastic order, was very plain – a reflection of the austerity of the order, founded in Florence in 1092 to restore the simplicity of monastic rule. A Baroque façade was added in 1593, but traces of its Romanesque predecessor can be seen on the interior east wall. The church contains superb examples of work by Ghirlandaio: frescoes of St Francis in the Sassetti Chapel (right of the High Altar) and the altar painting, *The Adoration of the Shepherds* (1485). These show what the church looked like in 1483–6 and include portraits of the donors of the chapel, Francesco Sassetti and his wife Nera Corsi, shown on either side of the altar. Sassetti was the general manager of the

The nave of Santa Trinità

Medici bank. The black sarcophagi of the Sassettis are by Giuliano da Sangallo.

Santi Apostoli 8

Map 5D. Piazza del Limbo. Open daily. Free.

The little Church of the Holy Apostles is, along with the Baptistry, among the oldest surviving churches in Florence. It has a simple Romanesque façade and the basilican plan typical of early Christian churches, but with 16th-century side aisles. Santi Apostoli fronts Piazza del Limbo, named for the cemetery once here, for infants who died before they could be baptized.

Della Robbia glazed terracotta tabernacle in Santi Apostoli

Ponte Vecchio 9

See pp40–1.

Palazzo Davanzati 10

Map 5D. Via Porta Rossa. Open daily except 1st, 3rd & 5th Mon, 2nd & 4th Sun of month.

Also called the Museo dell' Antica Casa Fiorentina, this is a typical 14th-century, lavish Florentine house.

Palazzo di Parte Guelfa 11

Map 5D. Piazza di Parte Guelfa. Closed to the public.

This characterful building served as the headquarters

The Roman-style triumphal arch, Piazza della Repubblica

of the Guelph party, who supported the Pope during the struggle for control over medieval Florence. The lower part of the building dates to the 13th century, but the upper part was added by Brunelleschi in 1431. Vasari made the open staircase, added in 1589.

Mercato Nuovo 🄬

Map 5E. Open daily Apr–Oct; open Tue–Sat Nov–Mar.

The Mercato Nuovo (New Market) is sometimes called the "Straw Market" because goods woven out of straw were once sold here. Today's stallholders sell leather goods and souvenirs.

Piazza della Repubblica 🄭

Map 4E.

Until 1890, this had been the site of the Mercato Vecchio (Old Market) and before

that of the ancient Roman forum. A single column from the old market still stands, and the Roman-style triumphal arch was built in 1895. The square is lined with pavement cafés, including the Giubbe Rosse. One of Florence's department stores, Rinascente, dominates the eastern side of the square.

One of the many pavement cafés in Piazza della Repubblica

Specialist shop in Via dei Fossi selling reproduction statuary

Palazzo Antinori 🄐

Map 4D. Piazza Antinori. Closed to the public.

The Palazzo Antinori, originally the Palazzo Boni e Martelli, was built in 1461–6. The Antinori family aquired it in 1506. The Cantinetta Antinori wine bar is a showcase for their produce.

Via dei Fossi 🄑

Map 4C.

The Via dei Fossi area contains some of the most absorbing shops in the city. Many of them specialize in antiques, works of art and statuary, reproduction marbles and classic Florentine products (like hand-made marbled papers, albums, notebooks and carnival masks), handwoven tapestries and rich Renaissance-style fabrics. Attached to the convent of the same name, the 16th-century frescoed Farmacia di Santa Maria Novella (Via della Scala) sells toiletries and liqueurs made by Dominican monks.

Museo Nazionale Alinari della Fotografia 🄰

Map 4C. Piazza Santa Maria Novella. Open daily. Adm charge.

The Alinari brothers began taking pictures of Florence in the 1840s, soon after the invention of photography. Their firm, set up in 1852, specialized in supplying top-quality prints, postcards and art books to tourists who flocked to the city at that time. Today, the archive provides a fascinating insight into the social history of Florence over the last 150 years.

Ognissanti 🄱

Map 4C. Borgo Ognissanti. Open daily except 1st & last Mon of month. Cenacolo del Ghirlandaio open Mon, Tue, Sat. Free.

The Church of All Saints, or Ognissanti, was the parish church of the Vespucci family, one of whom, Amerigo, gave his name to the New World. Amerigo is depicted in Ghirlandaio's fresco of the *Madonna della Misericordia* (1472) in the second chapel on the right. Sandro Botticelli is buried

The cloister of Ognissanti with 17th-century frescoes

here, and his fresco of *St Augustine* (1480) can be seen on the south wall, opposite Ghirlandaio's *St Jerome* (1480). Alongside the church are a cloister and refectory, containing Ghirlandaio's fresco *The Last Supper* (1480).

Santa Maria Novella

Map 3C. Piazza di Santa Maria Novella. Church open daily. Museum open Sat–Thu. Adm charge for both.

The Gothic Church of Santa Maria Novella was built by the Dominicans, from 1279 to 1357. The Renaissance façade, begun in 1458, was designed by Alberti. The chapels in the church contain some of the most important works of art in Florence, including frescoes and paintings by Masaccio, Filippino Lippi, Nardo di Cione, Ghirlandaio and Uccello. Beside the church is a cemetery walled in with *avelli* (grave niches), which

continue along the façade and the wall. The cloisters form a museum.

Frescoes in the Strozzi Chapel in Santa Maria Novella

Stazione di Santa Maria Novella

Map 2C. Open daily except 1.30–4.15pm.

A fine example of Italian "Functionalist" architecture, the central station was designed in 1935 by a collective of Tuscan artists, including Piero Berardi and Giovanni Michelucci.

STREET LIFE

RESTAURANTS

Il Latini
Map 4C. Via dei Palchetti 6r. Tel 050 210 916.
Moderate
All you can eat and drink of Tuscan stand-bys.

Cantinetta Antinori
Map 4D. Piazza Antinori 3. Tel 055 292 234.
Moderate
Wine bar-restaurant in the frescoed courtyard, of 15th-century Palazzo Antinori.

See page 80 for price codes.

BARS

Giubbe Rosse
Map 4E. Piazza della Repubblica 13–14r.
The waiters' giubbe rosse (red jackets) hark back to the glory days of Garibaldi. It is here that Florence's avant garde Futurists used to meet.

SHOPPING

Gucci
Map 4D. Via dei Tornabuoni 73r.
Former saddlemaker Guccio Gucci opened this leather-goods shop in 1904.

OLTRARNO

Oltrarno means "over the Arno", and living on the south bank of the river was once considered inferior. The Medici Grand Dukes moved here in 1550 and the Palazzo Pitti became their power base for the next 300 years. Over the years the Pitti increased almost threefold in size in comparison with the original plans, and the Boboli Gardens were laid out around it. In the late 16th and 17th centuries, many aristocrats built palazzi in the area surrounding Via Maggio and Piazza di Santo Spirito. Today, this is primarily a quiet area full of artisan workshops and antique shops, contrasting with the elegant palazzi and the unfinished austere façade of Santo Spirito.

SIGHTS AT A GLANCE

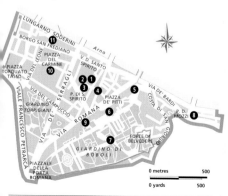

◀ *Rooftops of the Oltrarno and the spire and dome of Santo Sprrito*

Santo Spirito ❶

Map 5C. Piazza di Santo Spirito.
Closed for restoration.

Brunelleschi designed the church in 1435, on the site of an Augustinian foundation dating from 1250, but it was not completed until after his death in 1446. The 18th-century façade, which dominates the northern end of Piazza di Santo Spirito, is still unfinished. Inside, there is the Baroque baldacchino and the High Altar (1607), by Giovanni Caccini. The 38 side altars are decorated with 15th- and 16th-century Renaissance paintings and sculpture by Ghirlandaio, Rosselli and Lippi. In 1489, the sacristy was designed by Giuliano da Sangallo, and the adjoining vestibule, with

its ornate coffered ceiling, by Simone del Pollaiuolo (Cronaca) in 1491.

Cenacolo di Santo Spirito ❷

Map 5C. Piazza di Santo Spirito.
Open Tue–Sun (Sat only in winter) except 25 Dec, 1 Jan, Easter Sun, 1 May, 15 Aug. Adm charge.

All that survives of the monastery that stood next to Santo Spirito is the refectory (*cenacolo*), now a museum. Inside, a rare High Gothic fresco, *The Crucifixion* (1360–65), is attributed to the followers of Andrea Orcagna and his brother Nardo di Cione. The Fondazione Salvatore Romano, a collection of 11th-century Romanesque sculpture, is also on display.

Elegant colonnaded aisle in Santo Spirito

The façade of Palazzo Guadagni

Piazza di Santo Spirito ❸

Map 6C. Market: 2nd (Antiques) & 3rd (Organic) Sun of mth.

The biggest house on this medieval square is the Palazzo Guadagni at No. 10, on the corner with Via Mazzetta. It was built c.1505, probably to the designs of Cronaca. The top floor forms an open loggia, the first of its kind to be built in the city. It set a fashion among 16th-century aristocrats, and many incorporated the design into their own palazzi. Markets are held in the square twice a month.

Via Maggio ❹

Map 6C.

The grandest road in the district, the 13th-century Via Maggio became fashionable after the Medici Grand Dukes moved to the Palazzo Pitti in 1550. It is lined with 15th- and 16th-century palazzi and antique shops. Via Maggio runs into Piazza di San Felice, where a plaque marks the Casa Guidi. Elizabeth and Robert Browning, the English poets, rented an apartment here after eloping in 1847.

Santa Felicità ❺

Map 6D. Piazza di Santa Felicità. Open daily. Free.

A church has stood on this site since the 4th century AD, but the current building dates from the 11th century. In 1736–9, it was extensively remodelled by Ferdinando Ruggieri, but some original Gothic features, and the porch added by Vasari in 1564, were retained. The Capponi family chapel, to the right of the entrance, houses two masterpieces by Jacopo da Pontormo: *The Annunciation* and *The Deposition* (1525–8), both frescoes. Pontormo and his pupil Agnolo Bronzino also painted the roundels at the base of the ceiling vault.

Part of The Annunciation (1528) by Pontormo, in Santa Felicità

Boboli Gardens **❼**

The Boboli Gardens of the Palazzo Pitti were laid out for the Medici in 1550. A perfect example of stylized Renaissance horticulture, they comprise formal gardens of symmetrical box hedges and contrasting groves of wild ilex and cypress trees. The gardens were opened to the public in 1766.

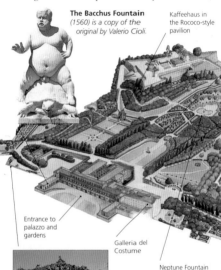

The Bacchus Fountain (1560) is a copy of the original by Valerio Cioli.

Kaffeehaus in the Rococo-style pavilion

Entrance to palazzo and gardens

Galleria del Costume

Neptune Fountain

La Grotta Grande, a Mannerist folly (1583–93), contains the casts of Michelangelo's Quattro Prigioni built into the walls.

The Amphitheatre was created from the hollow left after stone for the Palazzo Pitti was quarried.

L'Isolotto (Little Island) is home to Giambologna's Oceanus Fountain (1576).

Museo della Porcellane

Hemicycle (semi-circular lawn)

Entrance

The Orangery by Zanobi del Rosso was built in 1777–8 to protect rare plants from frost.

Viottolone, the avenue of cypress trees, is lined with Classical statues.

Ammannati designed inner court yard of Palazzo Pitti in 1560–70

Palazzo Pitti **6**

Map 6D. Piazza Pitti. Palatine Gallery & Royal Apartments open Tue–Sun. Galleria d'Arte Moderna, Galleria del Costume, Museo degli Argenti & Museo delle Porcellane open daily except 2nd, 4th Sun and 1st, 3rd & 5th Mon of month. All museums closed 25 Dec, 1 Jan, 1 May. Adm charge for each museum.

The Palazzo Pitti, begun in 1457, was originally built for the banker Luca Pitti. The façade is thought to be by Brunelleschi. A century later, the Medici bought it from Pitti's bankrupt heirs and, in 1550, it became the main Medici residence. Subsequently, all Florentine rulers lived here. Today, the rooms house treasures from collections of the Medici and the Dukes of Habsburg-Lorraine, who ruled after them. The frescoed walls of the Palatine Gallery, set up in the 1600s and 1700s, are hung with works from the Medici private collection, placed purely for effect, regardless of subject matter or chronology. Other attractions include the royal apartments, the Medici collection of jewellery and treasures in the Museo degli Argenti, the Galleria del Arte Moderna

(which houses modern art) and the Galleria del Costume, showing Italian clothing from the 18th, 19th and 20th centuries, which opened in 1983.

Boboli Gardens **7**

See pp50–1.

Museo Bardini **8**

Map 6F. Piazza de' Mozzi. Closed for restoration.

This 19th-century palazzo was built in 1883 by antiquarian and architectural salvager Stefano Bardini. The building is made almost entirely from recycled medieval and Renaissance masonry. The collection housed in it was left to the people of Florence in 1922.

Museo Bardini, Piazza de' Mozzi

Museo "La Specola" **9**

Map 6C. Via Romana. Open Thu–Tue except public hols. Adm charge.

"La Specola" refers to the observatory built on the roof of the building, the Palazzo Rottigiani, by Grand Duke Pietro Leopoldo in the late 18th century. It is now used by the natural science

faculty of the University of
Florence as a museum.

Brancacci Chapel 10

Map 5B. Piazza del Carmine.
Tel 055 276 85 58. Open Wed–
Mon except public hols (booking
required). Adm charge.

The chapel is part of the
Church of Santa Maria del
Carmine. It is famous for
The Life of St Peter frescoes
commissioned by the
Florentine merchant Felice
Brancacci. Masolino began
the work in 1425 but many
of the 12 scenes are by his
pupil, Masaccio (including
The Tribute Money), who
died before completing
the cycle. Filippino Lippi
finished the work in 1480.

San Frediano in Cestello 11

Map 5B. Piazza di Cestello. Open
daily. Free.

The large dome of the
parish church of San

The dome and plain façade of
San Frediano in Cestello

Frediano in Cestello is a
local landmark. The church
was rebuilt on the site of an
older one in 1680–89 by
Antonio Maria Ferri: the
interior frescos and stucco
work are typical of the peri-
od. The nearby Porta San
Frediano, built in 1324, has
a tower overlooking the
road to Pisa. Its wooden
doors have retained their
original 14th-century locks
and detailed ironwork.

STREET LIFE

RESTAURANTS

Il Cantinone
Map 5C. Via Santo Spirito 6r.
Tel 055 218 898.
Moderate
Crostini (grilled bread with
toppings) and more Tuscan
dishes at long wooden tables.

Alla Vecchia Bettola
Map 6A. Viale Vasco Pratolini
3/7. Tel 055 224 158.
Moderate
Where Florentines go to enjoy
some old-fashioned dishes –
including testicciole (rice stew
in a halved sheep's skull).

See page 80 for price codes.

BARS

Pitti Gola e Cantina
Map 6C. Piazza Pitti 16.
*A refined little wine bar with
very good snacks. It is situated
conveniently just across the
square from the Pitti Palace,
so a useful comfort stop after
all that art.*

SHOPPING

Pitti Mosaici
Map 6C. Piazza dei Pitti
23r–24r.
*Highest-quality pietre dure –
"mosaics" made from semi-
precious stones. Small pieces
make classy souvenirs. Closed
Sundays in winter.*

DAY TRIPS IN TUSCANY

Tuscany is full of fascinating places, but the following have been chosen because they make enjoyable days out for travellers based in Florence. Pisa and its tower are unmissable, as are the Piero della Francesca frescoes, now restored, in the San Francesco church at Arezzo.

SIGHTS AT A GLANCE

Historic Towns
Pisa ❶
Lucca ❻
Arezzo ❼
Siena ❽
San Gimignano ❾

National Parks and Resorts
Tenuto di San Rossore ❷
Marina di Pisa ❸

Churches and Monasteries
San Piero a Grade ❹
Certosa di Pisa ❺

SEE ALSO

• *Street Life pp61, 63, 67, 69, 73*

KEY

✈ Airport

| 0 km | 40 |
| 0 miles | 40 |

◀ *Fertile countryside surrounding Monterchi*

Pisa **❶**

Thanks to its powerful navy, Pisa dominated the Western Mediterranean from the 11th to the 13th centuries. Its splendid buildings date from this era. The city fell into decline when the Arno silted up, creating a salt marsh that divided it from the sea.

Campo dei Miracoli

① Campo dei Miracoli

See pp58–9.

② Museo delle Sinopie

Piazza del Duomo. Closed until further notice.

This fascinating museum houses sketches from the fresco cycle that covered the walls of Campo Santo cemetery *(see pp58–9)* before they were damaged by bombing in 1944.

③ Museo dell'Opera del Duomo

Piazza Duomo. Open daily. Adm charge.

The museum was opened in 1986. The exhibits come from the Duomo and Baptistry, including work by both Pisanos, paintings from the 15th to 18th centuries and Roman and ecclesiastical treasures.

Inlaid marble, Duomo façade

④ Piazza dei Cavalieri

The Piazza dei Cavalieri stands at the heart of Pisa's student quarter. The Palazzo dei Cavalieri, situated on the north side of the square, was designed in 1562 by Giorgio Vasari, as the headquarters of the Cavalieri di San Stefano, an order of knights created by Cosimo in 1561. Santo Stefano dei Cavalieri (1565–9), the knights' church, also by Vasari, stands next to the Palazzo. On the other side can be found the Palazzo dell'Orologio, incorporating the medieval town jail. In 1288 Count Ugolino, mayor of Pisa, was accused of treachery and walled up here with his sons.

⑤ Museo Nazionale di San Matteo

Piazzetta San Matteo in Soarta. Open Tue–Sun except 25 Dec, 1 Jan, 1 May, 15 Aug. Adm charge.

Housed in the medieval convent of San Matteo, the museum presents Pisan and Florentine art from the 12th to the 17th centuries. Most of the earliest works portray the Virgin and Child. These include Simone Martini's fine polyptych (1321) and a 14th-century statue, the *Madonna del Latte*, attributed to Nino Pisano. Also worth looking out for are Masaccio's *St Paul* (1426), Gentile da Fabriano's 15th-century *Madonna and Child* and Donatello's reliquary bust of *San Rossore* (1424–7).

⑥ Santa Maria della Spina

Lungarno Gambacorti. Open Tue–Sun. Free.

The church was built to house a thorn from Christ's Crown of Thorns. The roofline bristles with spiky Gothic pinnacles, spires and niches sheltering statues of apostles and saints.

⑦ San Paolo a Ripa d'Arno

Piazza San Paolo a Ripa d'Arno. Open by appt. Free.

This church was built in the same Pisan-Romanesque style as the Duomo *(see pp58–9),* and has a fine 12th-century façade. The Romanesque chapel is dedicated to St Agatha.

VISITORS' CHECKLIST

Airport: Galileo Galilei. Central station: Centrale, Viale Gramsci. Tourist information: Piazza Duomo, tel. 050 56 04 64. Market Wed, Sat. Shops closed Mon am.
www.pisa.turismo.toscana.it

PISA TOWN CENTRE

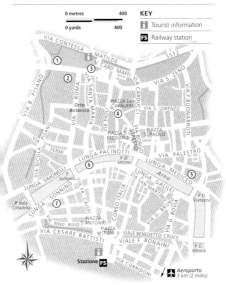

KEY	
🛈	Tourist information
FS	Railway station

Campo dei Miracoli

Pisa's Leaning Tower is just one of the religious buildings that rise from the emerald-green lawns of the Campo dei Miracoli, the "Field of Miracles". There is also the Duomo, begun in 1063, the Baptistry (1152–1284) and the Campo Santo cemetery begun in 1278. All the buildings show Moorish influence – and all lean, because their shallow foundations were set in sandy subsoil.

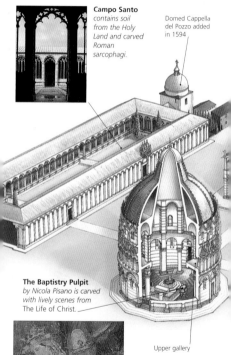

Campo Santo
contains soil from the Holy Land and carved Roman sarcophagi.

Domed Cappella del Pozzo added in 1594

The Baptistry Pulpit
by Nicola Pisano is carved with lively scenes from The Life of Christ.

Upper gallery

The Triumph of Death
is a cycle of late 14th-century frescoes depicting allegorical scenes.

The Duomo Façade, dating from the 12th century, is decorated with coloured sandstone, glass and majolica plates in inlaid marble.

The Leaning Tower was completed in 1350, when its seven bells were hung.

Frescoes added after a fire in 1595

Surviving fragments of the 11th-century marble floor

A Frieze shows that work began in 1173.

Wall tomb of Buscheto, the Duomo's first architect

Carrara marble walls

VISITORS' CHECKLIST

Piazza dei Miracoli. Duomo, Baptistry, Campo Santo and Campanile open daily (times depend on season). Adm charge (cumulative tickets available). Book admission time in advance.
www.opapisa.it

Giovanni Pisano's Pulpit Pulpit (1302–11) has carved supports that symbolize the Arts and Virtues.

The Leaning Tower of Pisa

No building on the Campo dei Miracoli tilts so famously as the Torre Pendente – the Leaning Tower. Begun in 1173, the tower began to tip sideways before the third storey was completed, but construction continued until its completion in 1350. The tilt has now been corrected by 38 cm (14 in).

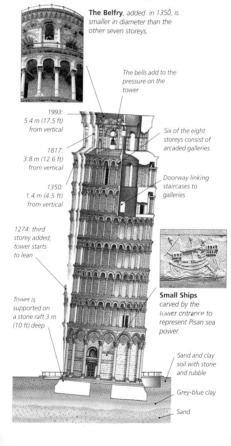

The Belfry, added in 1350, is smaller in diameter than the other seven storeys.

The bells add to the pressure on the tower

1993:
5.4 m (17.5 ft)
from vertical

1817:
3.8 m (12.6 ft)
from vertical

1350:
1.4 m (4.5 ft)
from vertical

Six of the eight storeys consist of arcaded galleries

Doorway linking staircases to galleries

1274: third storey added; tower starts to lean

Tower is supported on a stone raft 3 m (10 ft) deep

Small Ships carved by the lower entrance to represent Pisan sea power.

Sand and clay soil with stone and rubble

Grey-blue clay

Sand

Tenuta di San Rossore ❷

Open Sat, Sun, public hols. Free.

North of the Arno, this is
part of the Parco Naturale
di San Rossore, a nature
reserve stretching to the
north of Tuscany, where
wild boar roam. Gombo,
to the west, is where the
drowned body of the poet
Shelley was found in 1822.

Marina di Pisa ❸

There are extensive sandy
beaches on the Arno estu-
ary, and here lies Marina di
Pisa, a seaside resort with
some pretty Art Nouveau
houses backed by pine
woods. You may see grazing
camels, descendants of a
large herd established under
Duke Ferdinand II in the
mid-17th century.

San Piero a Grado ❹

Open daily. Free.

San Piero was built during
the reign of Pope John XVIII
(1004–9) on the spot where
St Peter is believed to have
first set foot on Italian soil in
AD 42. High up on the nave

Interior of San Piero a Grado, with frescoes by Deodati Orlandi

walls there are frescoes by
Deodato Orlandia, painted
around 1300 and depicting
The Life of St Peter.

Certosa di Pisa ❺

Open Tue–Sun. Adm charge.

This Carthusian monastery
was founded in 1366 and
rebuilt during the 18th century. The church is lavishly
decorated, and some parts
of the buildings form the
University of Pisa's Museo
di Storia Naturale.

STREET LIFE

RESTAURANTS	CAFÉS
Da Bruno Via Luigi Bianchi 12. Tel 050 560 818. **Moderate** *Excellent local dishes.*	**Caffè dell'Ussero** Lungarno Panicotti 27. *One of Italy's oldest literary cafes, dating from 1794. Great views over the Arno.*

RESTAURANTS	SHOPPING
Trattoria Sant'Omobono Piazza Sant'Omobono 6. Tel 050 540 847. **Moderate** *Gorgeous Pisan recipes.* *See page 80 for price codes.*	**Arturo Pasquinucci** Via Oberdan 22. *Classy contemporary Italian kitchenware from a traditional shop that opened in 1870.*

Lucca ❻

Lucca is enclosed by massive red brick walls built in 1504–1645. It is a city of narrow lanes, preserving intact its original ancient Roman street plan; it became a Roman colony in 180 BC. The Piazza del Mercato was once the city's amphitheatre. Lucca was the home of composer Giacomo Puccini.

Lucca viewed from the top of the Guinigi Tower

San Martino

See pp64–5.

Anfiteatro Romano

Piazza del Mercato.

Almost none of the ancient Roman amphitheatre survives, but you can see low archways at north, south, east and west that mark the gates through which beasts and gladiators would once have entered the arena.

Palazzo dei Guinigi

Via Sant'Andrea. Tower open daily except 25 Dec. Adm charge.

The Guinigi family palazzo, built in the late 14th century of red brick, has late-Gothic windows and an impressive 41-m (133-ft) defensive tower, the Torre del Guinigi.

Giardino Botanico

Via dell'Orto Botanico. Open Tue–Sun. Closed Sun (Nov–Mar). Adm charge.

Lucca's delightful botanical garden was laid out in 1820. It displays a wide range of Tuscan plants.

Museo della Cattedrale

Piazza Antelminelli. Open daily except 25 Dec, 1 Jan. Adm charge.

The 14th-century museum displays the treasures of the Duomo, San Martino, including the 11th-century carved stone head of a king from the original façade.

Museo Nazionale Villa Guinigi

Via della Quarquonia. Open Tue–Sun except 25 Dec, 1 Jan, 1 May. Adm charge.

This Renaissance villa was built for Paolo Guinigi, who ruled Lucca (1400 to 1430), keeping the city out of Medici clutches. The ground floor holds local sculpture and the gallery on the floor above displays paintings, furnishings and choir stalls from the cathedral.

Romanesque lion at Museo Nazionale Villa Guinigi

Piazza Napoleone and Piazza del Giglio

Piazza Napoleone was laid out in 1806 when Lucca was ruled by Elisa Baciocchi, Napoleon's sister, and contains the Palazzo Ducale. On the south side of the adjoining Piazza del Giglio is the Teatro del Giglio (1817), famous for its Puccini opera productions.

Casa di Puccini

Corte San Lorenzo. Closed until further notice.

The 15th-century birthplace of Giacomo Puccini (1858–1924) contains costume designs and the piano he used when composing his last opera, *Turandot*.

Museo Nazionale di Palazzo Mansi

Via Galli Tassi. Open Tue–Sun. Adm charge.

Lucca's art gallery, in the impressive 17th-century Palazzo Mansi, has works by Tintoretto, Andrea del Sarto, Bronzino, Pontormo, Sodoma and Salvatore Rosa.

Ramparts

Complete circuit: 4.2 km (2.5 miles).

You can walk round Lucca on the city walls, built in 1504–1645, using the promenade that runs along the top of them. Marie-Louise de Bourbon turned the ramparts into a public park in the early 19th century.

The Porta San Donato along the tree-lined ramparts walk

STREET LIFE

RESTAURANTS	CAFÉS
Da Leo Via Tegrimi 1. Tel 0583 492 236. **Cheap** Crowded with locals.	**Antico Caffè di Simo** Via Fillungo 58. Café of choice for musical and literary lights since 1846. Period interiors.

	SHOPPING
La Buca di Sant'Antonio Via della Cervia 3. Tel 0583 55 881. **Moderate** Lucca's classiest restaurant. See page 80 for price codes.	**Enoteca Vanni** Piazza Salvatore 7. Lucca's best wine shop, with hundreds of bottles crowded into small cellar rooms.

San Martino

Lucca's extraordinary cathedral, with its façade abutting incongruously on to the campanile, is dedicated to St Martin, the Roman soldier who divided his cloak with his sword to share with a needy beggar. It was built in the 13th century.

Romanesque blank arcades and carved capitals

Domed chapels encircling the apse

The Tomb of Ilaria del Carretto, *Paolo Guinigi's bride, by Jacopo della Quercia can be seen in the Sacristy.*

Volto Santo is a 13th-century effigy once believed to have been carved by Christ's follower Nicodemus, at the Crucifixion.

The Campanile *was built in 1060 as a defensive tower.*

The Gabled Façade *(1204) has three tiers of ornate colonnading.*

The Journey of the Magi and The Deposition *by Nicola Pisano can be seen here.*

Doorway Sculptures *include this 13th-century relief depicting the beheading of St Regulus.*

Arezzo ❼

One of the wealthiest cities in Tuscany, Arezzo is famous for Piero della Francesca's frescoes and for its antiques market. The Chimera fountain near the station, a copy of an Etruscan bronze cast here in 380 BC, is a reminder of the city's glorious past.

Chimera fountain

① Casa del Vasari

Via XX Settembre. Open Wed–Mon & public hols. Free.

Giovanni Vasari (1512–74) built this house in 1540 and decorated it with portraits of fellow artists and friends.

② Museo Statale d'Arte Medioevale e Moderna

Via di San Lorentino. Open Tue–Sun. Adm charge.

Housed in the 15th-century Palazzo Bruni, the collection includes work by Andrea della Robbia, Vasari, Signorelli and artists from the 19th and 20th centuries.

③ Museo del Duomo

Piazzetta behind the Duomo. Open Thu–Sat. Adm charge.

This houses treasures from the cathedral, including three wooden crosses from the 12th and 13th centuries, as well as frescoes by Vasari.

④ Duomo

Piazza del Duomo. Open daily. Free.

It contains 16th-century stained glass by Guillaume de Marcillat and a fresco of Mary Magdalene by Piero della Francesca (1410–92).

⑤ San Francesco

Piazza San Francisco. Tel 0575 35 27 27. Open daily (book ahead). Adm charge.

The 13th-century church of San Francesco contains one of Piero della Francesca's finest frescoes, *Legend of the True Cross* (1452–66).

⑥ Pieve di Santa Maria

Corso Italia. Open daily. Free.

The Pieve di Santa Maria has a splendid campanile, the "tower of a hundred holes."

⑦ Piazza Grande

The square is famous for its regular antiques market.

West side of Piazza Grande

⑧ Fortezza Medicea e Parco il Prato

Open daily. Free.

Sangallo's fortress was built in the 16th century.

⑨ Anfiteatro Romano e Museo Archeologico

Via Margaritone. Open daily except 25 Dec, 1 Jan, 1 May. Adm charge for museum.

The museum is famous for its Roman Aretine ware.

STREET LIFE

CAFÉ

Pasticceria Magi
Via Vittorio Veneto 65.
Cheap
Fresh coffee and good pastries.

SHOPPING

Antiques Market
Piazza Grande.
1st weekend of the month.
Over 600 dealers crowding the Piazza Grande.

Sotto San Francesco
Via S Francesco 5.
Wines, olive oils, also Aghiari lace and Monte San Savino ceramics by local artisans.

Unoaerre
Via Fiorentina 550.
Gold jewellery fusing modern technology with traditional craftsmanship.
See page 80 for price codes.

AREZZO TOWN CENTRE

KEY

- **i** Tourist information
- **FS** Railway station

Siena ❽

Siena is a city of steep medieval alleys surrounding the fan-shaped Piazza del Campo. The buildings around the square symbolize the golden age of the city (1260–1348), when wealthy citizens contributed to a major programme of civic building.

Siena's Piazza del Campo

① Fortezza Medicea

Viale Maccari. Fortezza open daily. Enoteca open Mon–Sat. Theatre open Nov–Apr: performances only.

Cosimo I's red-brick fortress, built in 1560, now houses a theatre and a wine shop.

② San Domenico

Piazza San Domenico. Open daily. Free.

Barn-like Gothic church with exquisite chapel (1460) dedicated to St Catherine.

③ Santuario e Casa di Santa Caterina

Costa di Sant'Antonio. Open daily. Free.

The house of Siena's patron saint, Catherine Benincasa (1347–80). It is decorated with paintings of her life.

④ Museo dell'Opera Metropolitana

Piazza del Duomo. Open daily except 25 Dec, 1 Jan. Adm charge.

Built into the unfinished side aisle of the Duomo, the museum holds the sculpture from the Duomo's exterior.

⑤ Siena Duomo

See pp70–1.

⑥ Piazza del Campo

The Palio, the bareback horse-race that is Tuscany's most celebrated festival, takes place here every year on 2 July and 16 August.

⑦ Palazzo Piccolomini

Via Banchi di Sotto. Open Mon–Sat except 1st two weeks in Aug. Free.

A private palazzo, built in the 1460s, that houses 13th-century municipal ledgers with covers by great artists.

⑧ Torre del Mangia

Piazza del Campo. Open daily except 25 Dec. Adm charge.

This belltower, built 1338–48 by the brothers Muccio and Francesco di Rinaldo is the second highest in Italy, at 102 m (330 ft).

VISITORS' CHECKLIST

Central Station: Piazza Stazione. Tourist information: Piazza del Campo, tel 0577 28 05 51. Market: Wed. **www**.terrasiena.it

⑨ Palazzo Pubblico

Piazza del Campo. Museo Civico open daily except 25 Dec. Adm charge.

The Palazzo Pubblico state rooms contain work by Renaissance artists and late 19th-century frescoes illustrating the events leading up to the unification of Italy.

⑩ Pinacoteca Nazionale

Via San Pietro. Open daily except 1 Jan, 1 May, 25 Dec. Adm charge.

Housed in the Palazzo Buonsignori, this gallery contains works by the Siena School, including Pietro da Domenico and a *Deposition* (1502) by Sodoma.

STREET LIFE	
RESTAURANTS	**BARS**
La Torre	**Nannini**
Via Salicotto 7.	Via Banchi di Sopra.
Tel 0577 287 548.	*Siena's renowned premier café.*
Cheap	
High-quality home cooking.	**Entoca I Terzi**
Fish is available on Fridays.	Via dei Termini 7.
	Wine bar serving Sienese dishes
See page 80 for price codes.	*under vaulted ceilings.*

SIENA TOWN CENTRE

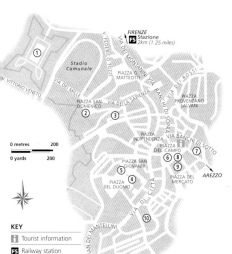

KEY

🛈 Tourist information

🚉 Railway station

Siena Duomo

Siena's Duomo (1136–1382) is one of the most spectacular in Italy, and one of the few south of the Alps in full Gothic style. A plan to build a new south nave came to nothing when plague hit the city. The unfinished nave contains a museum.

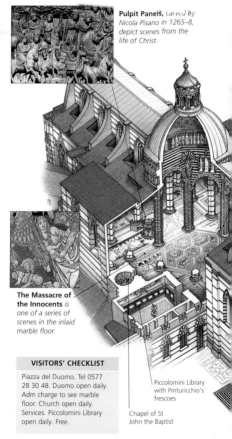

Pulpit Panels, *carved by Nicola Pisano in 1265–8, depict scenes from the life of Christ.*

The Massacre of the Innocents *is one of a series of scenes in the inlaid marble floor.*

VISITORS' CHECKLIST

Piazza del Duomo. Tel 0577 28 30 48. Duomo open daily. Adm charge to see marble floor. Church open daily. Services. Piccolomini Library open daily. Free.

Piccolomini Library with Pinturicchio's frescoes

Chapel of St John the Baptist

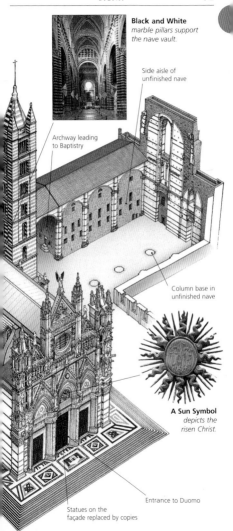

Black and White
*marble pillars support
the nave vault.*

Side aisle of
unfinished nave

Archway leading
to Baptistry

Column base in
unfinished nave

A Sun Symbol
*depicts the
risen Christ.*

Entrance to Duomo

Statues on the
façade replaced by copies

San Gimignano ❾

Tuscany's Manhattan, the "city of beautiful towers", San Gimignano is one of the best-preserved medieval towns in the region. Its stunning skyline bristles with tall towers dating from the 1200s with 14 of the original 76 having survived. They were built as private fortresses for their wealthy owners.

San Gimignano's skyline, almost unchanged since the Middle Ages

Palazzo Vecchio del Podestà

Piazza del Duomo. Closed to the public.

The Palazzo Vecchio del Podestà (the old Mayor's Palace) has a vaulted loggia and the 51-m (166-ft) Torre della Rognosa, one of the oldest towers in San Gimignano.

Museo Civico

Palazzo del Popolo, Piazza del Duomo. Museum, tower open daily. Adm charge.

The Museo is on the south side of the Piazza del Duomo, in the Palazzo del Popolo (town hall). Its tower, finished in 1311, is the tallest in the city, at 54 m (175 ft). Above the Sala di Dante, there is a small art collection, which includes Pinturicchio's *Madonna*

with Saints Gregory and Benedict (1511) and *San Gimignano and his Miracles* by Taddeo di Bartolo.

Museo d'Arte Sacra

Piazza Pecori. Open daily except four weeks in winter. Adm charge.

Access to the museum is via the Piazza Pecori. There are elaborate tomb slabs in the chapel, and the first floor houses paintings, sculpture and liturgical objects from the Collegiata.

Collegiata

Piazza del Duomo. Open daily except four weeks in winter. Adm charge.

The plain façade of this 12th-century Romanesque church disguises its fabulous interior. It is one of the most frescoed churches in Italy, containing work by Bartolo

The ceiling of the Collegiata, painted with gold stars

Old Testament), Lippo Memmi (the life of Christ) and Taddeo di Bartolo (*The Last Judgment*). In the tiny St Fina chapel, a cycle of frescoes by Ghirlandaio show the life story of the saint. His frescoes also grace the Baptistry loggia.

Rocca

Piazza Propositura. Open daily. Free.

The 1353 Rocca, or fortress, has only one surviving tower. It encloses a public garden of fig and olive trees, with views of vineyards.

Sant' Agostino

Piazza Sant'Agostino. Open daily. Free.

Consecrated in 1298, the church has a simple façade contrasting with Vanvitelli's Rococo interior (c.1740). Don't miss the *Coronation of the Virgin* (1483) by Piero del Pollaiuolo and the cycle of frescoes of *The Life of St Augustine* (1465) by Benozzo Gozzoli.

Detail from The Life of St Augustine

VISITORS' CHECKLIST

Bus station: Porta San Giovanni. Tourist information: Piazza del Duomo, tel 0577 94 00 08. Market: Thu. Shops closed Mon am. **www.sangimignano.com.**

STREET LIFE

RESTAURANTS

La Mangiatoria
Via Mainardi 5.
Tel 0577 941 528.
Moderate
"The Trough" is fun and lively.

Dorandò
Vicolo dell' Oro 2.
Tel 0577 941 862.
Expensive
Menus explain the ancient origins of each fine dish.

BARS

Bar I Combattenti
Via S. Giovanni 124.
Coffee and great home-made gelato on the main street.

SHOPPING

Enoteca la Botte e il Frantoio
Via S. Giovanni 56.
Sells Luciano Bruni's Varnaccia wine and Tuscan olive oil.
See page 80 for price codes.

Getting Around

Most cities in Tuscany are compact enough to get around on foot or by bus. Driving can be fraught, but it's the easiest way to explore Tuscany's back roads, hill towns and vineyards. Buses will take you to places that are inaccessible by train.

On Foot

A gentle stroll around the main sights of Florence can take just a couple of hours. The Duomo, Santa Maria Novella, Ponte Vecchio and the Accademia are all within ten minutes' walk of each other. Siena is compact but hilly, so wear sturdy shoes. The main sights in Pisa are all in the same square.

Automatic tollbooths on the motorway outside Florence

Stay on the pavement at all costs and then cross on green

Cycles or Mopeds

A day spent cycling in the countryside is relaxing, but mopeds or scooters make swifter work of the hills. Rentals are around €3 an hour for bicycles and €25 a day for mopeds. Ciclismo Classico and Experience Plus offer guided or self-guided bike trips.

Driving

City centres are a maze of one-way systems, limited traffic zones and erratic drivers. Visitors may go to their hotel within the city walls of Lucca, Siena and San Gimignano to unload luggage, but then must park outside the walls. It's usually cheaper to arrange car rental at home. Most filling stations close on Sundays, but many have automated machines that accept notes or credit cards.

Parking

A round blue sign with a red slash means no parking. Legal parking is always marked: white-line spaces are residential; yellow spaces off-limits; blue spaces by the hour, using pay-and-display or a scratch-off card from tobacconists (*tabacchi*).

Taxis

Official taxis are white in Tuscan cities. Take taxis at official ranks at airports or stations and your hotel.

Taxi at an offical rank in Florence

Travelling by Train

Florence's central railway station is Santa Maria Novella; Pisa has one in the centre, another at the airport. Siena's is outside the city walls on Piazzale Carlo Roselli, a 20-minute walk from the centre. Each station posts its own schedule (arrivals on white, departures on yellow) and newsstands sell national schedules. Buy a ticket before you travel. There are selfservice machines that take notes, coins or credit cards. For journeys under 200 km (124 miles), buy a shortrange ticket (*biglietto a fasce chilome-triche*). Stamp your ticket at the yellow machine before embarking.

An FS train at Florence station

Travelling by Coach (Bus)

Buses (pullman) are slower, but are best for getting to towns unreachable by train. In Florence, near Santa Maria Novella railway station, Lazzi, SITA, COPIT or CAP run extensive services within Tuscany. In Siena, TRA-IN runs local services from Piazza Antonio

Gramsci and regional buses from Piazza San Domenico. In Pisa, CPT buses serve the surrounding area from Piazza Sant'Antonio; Lazzi runs buses to Viareggio, Lucca and Florence from Piazza Vittorio Emanuele II.

Florence's main bus stop at Santa Maria Novella railway station

City Buses

All buses are bright orange. Lines run until at least 9:30pm, some until midnight or 1am in Florence. ATAF is Florence's city bus company, CPT in Pisa, TRA-IN in Siena. The useful routes in Florence are Nos. 7, 12, 13 and the A, B, C or D "eco-routes". Buy a ticket before boarding from tobacconists, bars, newsstands or bus termini. Tickets are valid for 70 minutes unlimited travel, or you can buy daily or weekly passes.

Travelling by Horseback

The romantic way to see Tuscany at a slow pace is in the saddle. For the Maremma in northern Tuscany, try Equitour or Il Paretaio.

TRAVEL INFORMATION

For information on trains:
www.trenitalia.it
Tel: 892 021

Survival Guide

Tuscany and its cities are generally safe, but pick-pockets are a common problem in Florence and Pisa, in crowded areas and on buses. Make sure you have travel insurance (including dental), as it is difficult to obtain once you are in the country.

MONEY

Exchange office at one of the national banks

Currency

The euro (€), the single European currency, operates in Italy. Euro banknotes have seven denominations from 5 to 500 and eight coin denominations from 1 cent to €2.

Banks

Banking hours are usually 8:30am–1:20pm, Mon–Fri. Most are open 2:45pm–4pm as well. They are closed on weekends and on public holidays (closing early the day before).

Euro Coin and notes

Credit Cards

MasterCard and VISA are the most popular, then American Express, then Diner's Card. Some banks and ATMs give credit card cash advances.

Changing Money

Always change money at a bank for the best rates and bring your passport as ID. Go to the window marked *cambio*, then to the *cassa* to obtain your euros. Use Cambio exchange booths outside banking hours.

ATMs

The fastest, easiest and cheapest way to get local currency is via an ATM (*bancomat*).

Traveller's Cheques

The safest way to carry money and are good in emergencies. Buy them in dollars or euros. Don't exchange at a shop or hotel, as the rate is poor.

COMMUNICATIONS

Post Offices

Italy's post is improving but is still very slow. Letters can take a few days or months. Buy stamps (*francobolli*) at newsstands, tobacconists or post offices (*ufficio postale*) for your destination; they know the correct amount. Drop it in the slot of the red post box, labelled *per tutte le altre destinazioni* (not *per la città*).

A tobacconist with red post box and telephone access

Telephones

Most pay phones in Italy accept only pre-paid phone cards (*scheda telefonica*). Buy them in denominations of € 5 or € 10 at tobacconists (*tabacchi*) or newsstands. To reverse the charges, dial the international operator on 170.

Internet Cafés

Internet rooms and cafés are popping up constantly. Hotels increasingly are installing a common-use computer with Web access.

HEALTH AND SAFETY

Police

Victims of crime should contact a police office (*questura*) for either local (*polizia*) or national (*carabinieri*) police.

Health Insurance

EU visitors should obtain a European Health Insurance Card before travelling, to receive free, emergency medical care. Non-EU visitors must have medical cover.

Hospitals and Doctors

Italian hospitals (*ospedale*) are semi-privatized. For urgent medical attention, go to the *Pronto Soccorso* (out-patients) of the nearest hospital:

• Tourist Medical Centre in Florence has a 24-hour on-call service and English-speaking doctors:
Tel: 055 47 54 11
• Florence Hospital
Tel: 055 275 81
• Siena Hospital
Tel: 0577 58 61 11
Associazione Volontari Ospedalieri have volunteer interpreters on call to help with medical matters.
Florence: 055 234 45 67
Siena: 0577 24 78 69

Dentists

Dentists in Italy are expensive. Find the nearest one in the yellow pages (*pagine gialle*).

Pharmacies

Pharmacies (*farmacies*) in Tuscany have a night rota (*servizio notturno*) and a Sunday opening rota posted on their doors. Florence has two 24-hour pharmacies:
• *Farmacia Comunale 13*, Santa Maria Novella station Tel: 055 21 67 61
• *Farmacia Molteni*, Via dei Calzaiuoli 7r
Tel: 055 28 94 90

Ambulance run by the Misericordia in Florence

EMERGENCY NUMBERS

Ambulance
Tel: 118
Police
Tel: 112
General SOS
Tel: 113

Index

Acknowledgments

Dorling Kindersley would like to thank the following people whose help and assistance contributed to the preparation of this book.

Design and Editorial

Publisher Douglas Amrine
Publishing Manager Vivien Antwi
Managing Art Editor Kate Poole
Cartography Casper Morris
Design Kavita Saha, Shahid Mahmood
Editorial Dora Whitaker
Production Controller Shane Higgins
Picture Research Ellen Root
DTP Jason Little
Jacket Design Simon Oon, Tessa Bindloss
Beverley Ager, Mariana Evmolpidou, Anna Freiberger, Rebecca Milner, Marianne Petrou

Picture Credits

Every effort has been made to trace the copyright holders, and we apologize in advance for any omissions. We would be pleased to insert appropriate acknowledgments in any subsequent edition of this publication.

t = top; tl = top left; tc = top centre; tr = top right; cla = centre left above; ca = centre above; cra = centre right above; cl = centre left; c = centre; cr = centre right; clb = centre left below; cb = centre below; crb = centre right below; bl = bottom left; b = bottom; bc = bottom centre; br = bottom right.

Works of art have been reproduced with permission of the following copyright holders: *Cavaliere* (1949) Marino Marini © DACS, London 2006 38tl.

The Publishers are grateful to the following individuals, companies and picture libraries for permission to reproduce their photographs:

Bridgeman Art Library: Santa Croce, Firenze 16b; Instituto e Museo Storia della Scienza, Firenze: 15f; Museo Dell'Opificio delle Pietre Dure, Firenze: 33cl; Scala: 34br; Badia, Firenze 11tl; Corridoio Vasariano 40cr; Duomo, Lucca 64br; Galleria degli Uffizi, Firenze 25t; The Travel Library 32b.

Jacket
Front – Robert Harding Picture Library: Roy Rainford; Spine – DK Images: John Heseltine

All other images © Dorling Kindersley
For further information see www.DKimages.com.

Price Codes are for a three-course meal per person including tax, service, cover charge and half a bottle of house wine
Cheap under €15
Moderate €15–€40
Expensive €40 or more

SPECIAL EDITIONS OF DK TRAVEL GUIDES

DK Travel Guides can be purchased in bulk quantities at discounted prices for use in promotions or as premiums. We are also able to offer special editions and personalized jackets, corporate imprints, and excerpts from all of our books, tailored specifically to meet your own needs.

To find out more, please contact:
(in the United States)
SpecialSales@dk.com
(in the UK) **Sarah.Burgess@dk.com**
(in Canada) DK Special Sales at **general@tourmaline.ca**
(in Australia) **business.development@pearson.com.au**

Phrase Book

In Emergency

Help!	**Aiuto!**	*eye-yoo-toh*
Stop!	**Fermate!**	*fair-mah-teh*
Call a doctor.	**Chiama un medico**	*kee-ah-mah oon meh-dee-koh*
Call an ambulance.	**Chiama un' ambulanza**	*kee-ah-mah oon am-boo-lan-tsa*
Call the police.	**Chiama la polizia**	*kee-ah-mah lah pol-ee-tsee-ah*
Call the fire brigade.	**Chiama i pompieri**	*kee-ah-mah ee pom-pee-air-ee*
Where is the telephone?	**Dov'è il telefono?**	*dov-eh eel teh-leh-foh-noh?*
The nearest hospital?	**L'ospedale più vicino?**	*loss-peh-dah-leh pee-oovee-chee-noh?*

Communication Essentials

Yes/No	**Sì/No**	*see/noh*
Please	**Per favore**	*pair fah-vor-eh*
Thank you	**Grazie**	*grah-tsee-eh*
Excuse me	**Mi scusi**	*mee skoo-zee*
Hello	**Buon giorno**	*bwon jor-noh*
Good bye	**Arrivederci**	*ah-ree-veh-dair-chee*
Good evening	**Buona sera**	*bwon-ah sair-ah*
here/there	**qui/là**	*kwee/lah*
What?	**Quale?**	*kwah-leh?*
When?	**Quando?**	*kwan-doh?*
Why?	**Perchè?**	*pair-keh?*
Where?	**Dove?**	*doh-veh*

Useful Phrases

How are you?	**Come sta?**	*koh-meh stah?*
Very well, thank you.	**Molto bene, grazie.**	*moll-toh beh-neh grah-tsee-eh*
Pleased to meet you.	**Piacere di conoscerla.**	*pee-ah-chair-eh dee coh-noh-shair-lah*
See you soon.	**A più tardi.**	*ah pee-oo tar-dee*
That's fine.	**Va bene.**	*va beh-neh*
Where is/are ...?	**Dov'è/Dove sono ...?**	*dov-eh/doveh soh-noh?*
Do you speak English?	**Parla inglese?**	*par-lah een-gleh zeh?*
I don't understand.	**Non capisco.**	*non ka-pee-skoh*
Could you speak more slowly, please?	**Può parlare più lentamente, per favore?**	*pwoh par-lah-reh pee-oo len-ta-men-teh pair fah-vor-eh*

Useful Words

big	**grande**	*gran-deh*
small	**piccolo**	*pee-koh-loh*
hot	**caldo**	*kal-doh*
cold	**freddo**	*fred-doh*
open	**aperto**	*ah-pair-toh*
closed	**chiuso**	*kee-oo-zoh*
left	**a sinistra**	*ah see-nee-strah*
right	**a destra**	*ah dess-trah*
straight on	**sempre dritto**	*sem-preh dree-toh*
entrance	**entrata**	*en-trah-tah*
exit	**uscita**	*oo-shee-ta*
toilet	**il gabinetto**	*eel gab-bee-net-toh*